100 IDEAS
FOR MANAGING BEHAVIOUR

CONTINUUM ONE HUNDREDS SERIES

OTHER BEHAVIOUR TITLES

100 IDEAS
FOR MANAGING
BEHAVIOUR

Johnnie Young

continuum
LONDON • NEW YORK

This book is dedicated to my wife Sylvie
and my three children Edward
(and his partner Jade), Julie and William.
They have been with me all the way.

Continuum International Publishing Group

The Tower Building   15 East 26th Street
11 York Road   New York
London   NY 10010
SE1 7NX

www.continuumbooks.com

British Library Cataloguing-in-Publication Data

A catalogue record for this book is available from the British
Library.

ISBN: 0–8264–8477–8 (paperback)

Designed and typeset by Ben Cracknell Studios | Janice Mather

Printed and bound in Great Britain by MPG Books Ltd,
Bodmin, Cornwall

CONTENTS

SECTION 3 **Keeping things on track in the classroom**

ACKNOWLEDGEMENTS

First of all I would like to thank my publishers, Continuum, and in particular Alexandra Webster for her vision in seeing the potential of my original idea and Christina Parkinson who has been wonderful in her guidance, patience and support all along the way.

There are dozens of teachers who, over the years, have taught me so much. I would like to thank my friend and colleague William Barnard for his indispensable advice and support. I would like to thank John Holt for believing in me. Bob Penefold is a genius, unforgettable and a much-loved inspiration to me and many others (particularly students with challenging behaviour!). David Pryke taught me when I was a student and became a colleague and great friend. Thank you. I would like also to thank Jayne Blenkarn, the best head of department and the hardest worker I know. From the teachers of the distant past who taught me when I was a student I would like to thank Tony Ranson for inspiring me in English, Chris Young (no relation) for inspiring me in drama, my brother Derek who taught me to read in the early days, my brother Brian who is a natural and clear communicator and last of all, the greatest teacher I ever knew, my mother, for inspiring me in life! Thank you all.

INTRODUCTION

I started teaching straight after leaving a management position in a bank. I had been with the bank for sixteen years but had dreamed of being a teacher all my life. I wanted to influence a whole generation of students. I had studied part-time to get an Open University Honours Degree in English Literature; had taught staff in the bank; and had held evening adult education classes for some time. So with confidence I strode into my first school who had kindly agreed to try me out on an unqualified basis.

And so it was that I was led to my first classroom where a Year 9 middle-ability class waited. 'Today we're going to study a poem,' I importantly announced to the class. 'What's a poem?' came a shouted reply. The next hour was the worst of my life. All I could think was: 'What have I done?' I started training to become a 'licensed teacher'. I attended university once a week for two years and was observed in my classroom environment on countless occasions.

My lessons were, quite frankly, a battleground. True, I knew my subject. I knew it well. But the problem was I didn't know how to teach it. The classes were bored with me. I shouted all lesson. I gave handfuls of detention slips. I ended each lesson exhausted and depressed. I started considering a completely different line of work. I really didn't know what to do.

I realized that when I observed lessons of experienced teachers some seemed to do much better than others. I began asking these teachers lots of questions and I recorded their answers in a notebook (this was to be the first of many notebooks). I realized I thought I knew how to teach, but I really would have to start from scratch. I made it a habit to record helpful tips from experienced teachers. 'What do you do if they want to go to the toilet?' I would ask. 'If you let one go they all want to go. If you say no they might wee themselves.' 'Tell them to wait ten minutes and if it's still an emergency let them go,' came the reply. Into my notebook it went.

Over the years I filled dozens of notebooks with thousands of ideas. I still do. That is the great thing about teaching. You never stop learning. As I became more experienced I started to come up with my own ideas and adapted old ones. If I had a particularly good lesson I would reflect on why it was good. I noted down the essence of the reason why.

I have noticed, with regret, that a lot of staff in education have given up the ghost and left the profession feeling disillusioned. I have been teaching now for 12 years. I didn't leave because I realized that like any craft there is a knack to doing it. I have not always had brilliant lessons. No teacher can ever claim that. But as I've learnt more about the craft of teaching and tried to put the ideas into practice I have enjoyed the experience more and more, and I think my students have too.

I have extracted the best 100 ideas from my notebooks for dealing with students with challenging behaviour. When I began teaching I wish I could have got my hands on a book which gave practical tips on how to teach more effectively. I used to despair at the thickly laid academic texts that seemed to bear no relation to the classroom experience. This is why I've turned my ideas into this book to help new, and I hope experienced, teachers. The beauty of these ideas is that they are all tried and tested in a classroom environment. Some include actual examples of the words a teacher may use in a particular situation. There are comments designed to make teachers aware of risk areas and there are many strategies offered for teaching students with challenging behaviour.

I hope that in a small way my book will inspire teachers to give the best of themselves and to get the best from their students. Here it is. I hope you like it.

Johnnie Young   xi

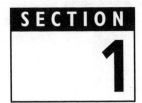

Getting to know them …

KNOWING THEIR NAMES

The first few lessons with a challenging class can be extremely difficult as you struggle, under pressure, to learn your students' names. To learn their names quickly try one or all of the following:

- Seat them alphabetically as they appear in the register.
- Ask them to make simple signs out of A4 paper with their name clearly written on. They should keep this in front of them until you're confident as to who's who.
- Ask them to bring in passport photographs of themselves which you stick to a seating plan next to their names.

If these are students in Year 8 or upwards it's useful to talk to teachers who taught them in previous years. They may have useful advice on how to deal with particularly difficult students or classes.

Build up a profile of your students' interests. It will take time and patience but persevere because it's an investment that will pay huge dividends.

If, for example, they have to write a story, students will often complain they can't think what to write about. In response the teacher may suggest several options, none of which inspires the student. How much better to be able to say:

> *'Imagine you're fishing (you know the student loves fishing) and you catch a huge one. When you reel it in you are amazed at what you find . . . Continue the story . . . '*

You will find that this is much more effective than a blanket 'write about anything' approach.

USING THEIR LIFE TARGETS TO MOTIVATE

Following on from Idea 2, keep building a profile of each student and gradually you'll get a picture of what they want to do in life. This information is very useful as you can raise students' interest levels by linking the subject matter to their personal interests.

For example, you're trying to teach an uninterested student how to produce a colour chart in an art lesson. If you know he or she wants to be a hairdresser you can ask him or her to design a chart of different hair colours, or to design the colours into different hairstyles.

In practice it's not, of course, possible to do this sort of thing with every student in every lesson. However, as part of your 'toolkit' to tackle certain problems it can be a wonderful way to motivate students into doing good, meaningful work.

Students with challenging behaviour often have low self-esteem and little regard for the value and worth of their work.

When a student produces work it's important to be honest and specific about how it could be improved. Remember to always show that you value his or her efforts and point out something that's been done well. You may be the only person in that student's life who has the chance to give positive feedback.

At first you may come up against certain students who disbelieve your apparent appreciation of their work. Don't give up! Appreciate every improvement no matter how small. Show students how they're improving by comparing work done now to work from several weeks ago. In time you will win over their trust and your comments will be important to them. This is a long, hard process and they'll know if you're not sincere.

Finally, remember that however badly a lesson goes, next lesson spring back and be enthusiastic about their work again. They will soon get used to your indomitable style!

ELEVATING THE IMPORTANCE OF STUDENTS' WORK

USING HUMOUR

A great way of dealing with students and creating a better classroom atmosphere is to use humour. However, there are two things you should be careful of.

1 Don't use humour until you're confident you have control over the class. Misplaced humour can cause the very trouble you were seeking to avoid.

2 Be aware that although it may not show, particularly with badly behaved students, they're at a very sensitive and self-conscious age. A comment designed to create a harmless giggle at the size of a student's nose could have a really disastrous set of consequences.

Safer ground is to never make a personal comment about a student, even in jest, and to stick to either making fun of yourself or the topic you're studying. Once you've made a joke try and get the class back to the task at hand as soon as possible.

There is a tendency, particularly with new teachers, to be too friendly with students. When adults interact they do so in a friendly manner to ensure smooth relationships. It's natural to assume that by being friendly to students you'll get the best out of them. But be careful. You are not a friend to the student: you're their teacher. One of your most important roles is to lead and organize their learning environment. If you are too friendly many students will not do as you ask them, and with challenging students this can become a disaster.

The main tip here is to think long term. It's not just one lesson you need to think about. You're attempting to build a long-term relationship where each time you meet the student you help them progress in their learning. If you're too strict you risk coming up against confrontation straight away. If you're too friendly the students will see you as a soft touch.

It's best, therefore, to work out your own rules of engagement. Develop your individual classroom personality and try and pitch it between the two extremes mentioned above. Always be consistent with your approach. Once the students are familiar with your rules of engagement they will work within them and know when they step outside of them. The students prefer this because they know clearly where they stand and what to expect from you.

FRIEND OR FOE?

IDEA

7

YOUR ATTITUDE HELPS

If you listen to comments made by students about teachers they don't like you often hear this: 'He's miserable.'

If you always have an interested, friendly, upbeat attitude and you are consistent with it (this should all be part of the Rules of Engagement set up in Idea 6); you will find this has a huge effect on the attitude of your students. You're setting the tone, and you'll need resilience to keep bouncing back with this upbeat feel.

If you feel fed up before a lesson pretend to be happy for about five or ten minutes. A remarkable thing happens: you do become happy.

A great way to get to know your students and to have some fun in the lesson is to have a 'star of the match' system.

Each lesson tell the students that you're going to pick a 'star', and that there are a range of reasons why an individual may be chosen. It may be an improvement

○ in effort;
○ in quality of work;
○ in attitude to work.

Ask the students how they're progressing with their work and be very encouraging of signs of improvement. You'll find that students compete in order to show you they're doing well.

Announce at the end of the lesson who the star is, and specifically what it is they've done to gain the title. Remind the other students that it could be them next time around. Every lesson a student will be chosen and, human nature being what it is, everyone takes an interest. When it works well the students become keen to offer up suggestions about themselves to gain them the coveted title!

To reinforce what it is you're looking for, maintain a chart on the wall with the names of the stars and the reasons and dates. Of course a student can win more than once.

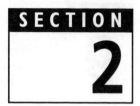

How to keep cool when the going gets tough

THE POWER OF ORGANIZATION

Imagine the situation below.

Sophie demands a pen and starts shouting for one. She grabs at Henry's who swears back at her. You search frantically for a spare pen to settle the argument. You can't find one. While your nose is buried in your briefcase a fight breaks out. In desperation you have to lend her your own expensive one.

Every teacher has been in a similar situation. The key to avoiding it is pure and simple: organization. Try to set aside regular time to plan your organization in detail. Think out exactly what you'll need and make a master checklist for each class. Into each class you should take:

○ one case with your master records;
○ spare stationery;
○ the correct number of worksheets or textbooks;
○ anything special for the activities planned.

If you do this life will be easier and you'll increase the chances of a good, smooth lesson.

Creating an encouraging atmosphere by using positive language is a great habit to get into. For example, instead of saying:

'I told you to be quiet, now I'm getting annoyed!'

You should say:

'Excellent! Most people are becoming quiet. Just a few more and we're there.'

This approach anticipates the results you require and produces a positive atmosphere. You can adapt this to any instructions and any type of behaviour. The tone of the voice may well be firm but the message is saying: 'Good, we're getting there!'

POSITIVE INSTRUCTIONS

IDEA

11

STOP SHOUTING

If a teacher has done all they can to get the attention of a class, but the class is still messing about, then it seems natural to start shouting. But what do you do when you shout and the class still takes no notice of you?

When I first started teaching I used to shout a lot and I found that it wore me out and didn't really help much. What was worse was that my voice was damaged and that made the next lesson harder. Over the years I've developed a number of strategies and techniques which remove the need to shout.

○ Stand and wait with a certain 'look'(see Idea 14 for more on this).
○ Lower your voice so that students have to listen harder to hear you.
○ Stop half way through a sentence or word and glare for a second at the person talking. This is a great method but you must practice to get the timing just right so it doesn't draw a comment from the student.
○ Hold your hand in the air and wait for silence.

The strategic shout also works amazingly well. Try the above techniques first but if somebody is still messing about shout just one word like 'Right!' and then go straight back to your lower voice. This technique protects your voice and, if the strategic shout is correctly timed and directed in the right way, it can work much better than shouting for most of the lesson.

There is a lot of information available about body language and how our own communicates a lot about us. In a classroom, body language and your awareness of it is vital. I have identified some key practical tips below which are useful when it comes to managing challenging behaviour.

Remember that from the moment you enter the classroom you're on show. Thirty pairs of observant eyes are watching and assessing you and they're looking for clues. Are you soft? Are you nervous? Do you know what you're doing? Are you experienced? This is the type of information you are constantly broadcasting with your body language. Remember to:

○ look and act confidently;
○ stand upright, do not hunch;
○ keep your eyes scanning the group;
○ show at all times that you're well aware of what is going on by broadcasting your observations;
○ develop signals to indicate desired actions (see Idea 13 for more details)
○ move about confidently;
○ have your records to hand and don't mess around in a briefcase where you cannot watch the class;
○ when pointing to the board or visuals be clear and definite;
○ have a hotspot where you stand from which you almost always give instructions;
○ sometimes stand at the back of the classroom – if a student turns round to see what you're doing point back to their work and continue to stand confidently;
○ always be aware of how you move – don't rush or get flustered.

THE BEAUTY OF SIGNALS

Often teachers talk too much and students will not take on board a lot of what's said (although they seem to have developed wonderful ways of looking like they are listening!).

By building up a simple language of symbols, you'll talk less and conserve energy. Here are four examples which have worked well for me.

1 Putting your hand up in the air at the beginning of the lesson, or whenever you require the students to listen, while you hold a prominent finger to your lips is a good way to get them to listen without you having to shout.
2 If a student is not working, point back to his or her book.
3 If a student has not removed a hat or coat, simply mime tugging gently at your own and then point to theirs.
4 A lot of instructions, particularly those which start the lesson can be written on the board, for example: 'Write this title and copy this sentence.'

There are many more examples and you will find the ones that work best for you. The key is to be consistent and to keep the silent signals clear and simple. Use them often and the students will recognize them and cooperate. Apart from anything else, you will ease the strain on your voice!

In the teacher's armoury 'the look' is of great importance. It is a good idea to practise this on your own beforehand. Basically, it's a way of showing, without words, that you're not happy. It works extremely well if you perfect it and use it appropriately, but don't overuse it.

For example, if you're interrupted while explaining something to the class, stop half way through a sentence and stare at the student responsible. You must get your timing right for this. To stare for too long will invite an unwelcome comment, to stare for too short a time will not have a powerful enough effect. As you look at the student say to yourself, 'one thousand and one, one thousand and two, one thousand and three,' then look away and carry on with what you were saying. I can guarantee that you'll find this is a highly effective technique.

DEVELOPING 'THE LOOK'

IDEA 15

When students are impolite to you, you must remain polite, calm and quietly spoken in return. This way, you are constantly reminding the students that:

'I'm being polite to you and I would like you to be polite to me.'

By keeping to these standards you will wear them down with your politeness and they will respect you for it. This ties in with your classroom attitude discussed in Idea 7.

I keep coming back to this because it's so important. Be consistent!

When dealing with students with challenging behaviour, consistency is vital as the students soon get to know if you really do mean what you say. The point of a consistent approach is to decide upon your parameters. Setting unrealistic goals with homework for students with low motivation means they'll never be achieved. Giving too many detentions is exhausting for you to follow up. Too many offers of letters home might be difficult to deliver. Work out reasonable parameters, but then make sure you maintain them, for example:

○ when giving sanctions make sure that what you threaten to do you actually carry out;
○ if you promise to write a letter home to acknowledge good work then make sure you do it;
○ if you have to resort to keeping a student in detention make sure that come what may that student ends up in detention;
○ if you're chasing outstanding homework don't give up until you've got it.

Over a period of time a professional consistent approach, where the students see that you never fall down on what you say, will build up a long-term trust and will help you enormously in managing your class.

THE POWER OF CONSISTENCY

BEING GENTLE

When faced with a lot of students with challenging behaviour in one class it's all too easy to become annoyed and angry, especially when your carefully prepared lesson starts to fall apart.

It is a useful tip when under such stress to have a mental trigger word like 'gentle' which will remind you, at the time you most need it, to maintain a calm, gentle and persistent approach. Whatever you do, don't get rattled. If you do, the students (who, don't forget, are experts at rattling teachers) will latch on to that and go for you like hyenas stalking an injured lion!

Pretend to be calm. Say confident things like: 'Good, most of the class are working. I'm pleased with that. Now you girls there, a bit more effort please!' Phrases like this give strong messages around the room that you're confident, calm and in control. Stay gentle and persistent and you will win through.

Some students with challenging behaviour will be very skilful at dragging you into an argument. For example, a student may argue with you and then try to pull in support from his or her friends. A good counter balance to this is to use 'deflection'. This is where you acknowledge what the student says and then deflect attention straight back on to the work. You may have to do this several times. It is also a good idea to focus attention onto another student who you know is working well.

This is a great tactic as it means you don't ignore the disruptive student but you also don't engage in an argument, which will disrupt the progress of the lesson. If you're careful and persistent with this technique you'll find it can be very useful in keeping the behaviour of the class on track.

USING DEFLECTION

IDEA 19

YOUR REACTIONS

It is really useful to think about your reactions to various problems before they arise. Although it's impossible to run through possible reactions to every situation, below is a list of common problems.

Think about how you would react in each given situation and plan an appropriate response.

o Late arrival to your class.
o Notes being passed around.
o Mobile phones being used.
o Homework not being delivered on time.
o Missing pens/pencils/work, etc.

Having your reaction planned will give you a greater sense of confidence and makes you look more on the ball. Keep a brief note in your record book about how you did react to problems as they arose, noting what you did right and how you think you may have handled the situation better. This will help you to plan ahead.

In a tired moment your lesson can be ruined by one comment you haven't thought through.
It's very easy to do and can cause lots of trouble. A student will capitalize on this situation and the problem can escalate with other students needing no encouragement to join in with the ensuing mayhem. In your attempt to redirect their attention back to the work you'll find you're swimming against a tide of disruption.

The thing to remember is that a classroom is a stressful environment where you have to have your wits about you. The tip therefore is to get into the habit of thinking about the effect of what you're going to say before you actually say it. It sounds so obvious but it's surprising how often teachers forget to do this.

THE WISDOM OF THINKING TWICE

IDEA

21

MAGIC PHRASES

Below are some excellent phrases I've used with students with challenging behaviour.

○ To get attention, hold up an object and say: 'Can anyone in this room tell me what this is?'

○ To warn about a sanction: 'Right, I don't usually have to do this but you leave me no choice.'

○ To get more hands up in response to a question: 'Come on, only three people can answer this? Surely not? Come on, let's have some more!'

○ To quieten a class: 'I'm asking you politely.'

○ To get the general noise level down: 'I would like the noise level down please. Five, four, three, two, one!'

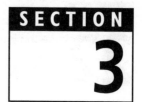

Keeping things on track in the classroom

IDEA 22

TALK UP THE CLASS

At the start of the lesson recount the good points of the last lesson. I find that mentioning specific instances of improvement as students come through the door really acts as a boost to their confidence. For example, you could congratulate:

o Drew for arriving on time to lessons;
o Matthew for staying in his seat more;
o Helen for an overall improvement in presentation.

Emphasize how happy you are with their progress. By doing this on a regular basis, you talk the class up and create a good relationship with them. It also gives the message that you're always looking out for improvements, however slight.

It can be difficult to start a lesson. Often the whole group seems completely uninterested in anything. So, how do you awaken their desire to get started? A great way to do this is to remind the class of the really good things they did in the last lesson. In particular, pick out the names of students who did well (try not to always pick the same people!) and encourage them to do even better in the current lesson. For example:

○ 'Meera – well done on completing the written task last lesson. I'm sure you'll do well at today's task.'
○ 'Jack – you managed to understand "x" concept last lesson. Let's see how well we can build on that this lesson.'

The great thing about this technique is that it anticipates a good lesson. Many teachers start off with a moan, and I've even seen teachers writing names on the board for detention at the beginning of the lesson – this is a big mistake!

With this method you quickly set up a strong sense of success and because it's based on the last lesson it makes everyone feel confident that they can achieve at least as well as last time.

Of course, to get the best from this you must remember to keep good outline notes of what happened in each lesson and highlight which students did particularly well.

Once you have delivered this upbeat message you can launch straight into your starter.

HOW TO 'SUPER-START' A LESSON

IDEA 24

A great way to involve students right at the start of the lesson, and therefore minimize opportunities for poor behaviour, is to have a set of flash cards ready with answers to simple questions with one-word answers written on them. For example, 'What is the capital of France?' It's good to use A4 cards with large lettering and it works well if the cards are in a variety of different, bright colours.

Hand the cards to students as they come in and then start asking them questions. To reply they must hold up the correct card. For example, the student who has Paris would hold up their card in response to the question mentioned above. You can of course adapt the questions for any subject. It has the advantage of:

o involving the students straight away in the lesson and focusing their attention on you;
o giving them something physical to do;
o being easy for them as no writing is required;
o allowing them to respond without talking.

Although it seems straightforward, handing out materials can cause chaos. To minimize disruption have a carefully worked out system in place.

Don't give out work yourself as it's when your back is turned that problems emerge. Instead, have a rota of monitors recorded on your seating plan. With monitors you can stand at the front and command the situation – it's a bit like directing the traffic!

○ Make sure that your monitors have a particular row or group which they work to.
○ Always insist that the students put their pens down and listen carefully before work is collected in.
○ Make sure that you allow plenty of time to do this to avoid rush and chaos when the bell goes.

Explain exactly how you want the work before it's collected in. For example:

'Please close your exercise books and put the blue sheet next to it. Take the green sheet home for homework. Now monitors, please listen carefully. Collect in a neat pile the exercise books from your row and a set of blue sheets. Right, collect them in now please.'

If you stick to this system of rota and monitors the students will get used to it and it will save you a lot of time and trouble.

THE MAGIC THREE

Rather than making the whole class do the same task, try giving them a choice of three tasks. These can be clearly set out on the white board. Give the class time to decide and then ask them to write their choice in their books. Now as they start their tasks you can go around the class to check what they've chosen.

I find that there's something about giving this choice of tasks which makes the work more attractive to the students (they like the feeling of autonomy). But beware, if you have more than three choices it can sometimes lead to a 'spoilt for choice' situation whereupon no task is actually chosen.

To help the logistics of this idea I find that three piles of colour-coded worksheets helps to start the students working. For example, on the board it will indicate: 1 = blue sheet; 2 = orange; 3 = green.

Sometimes it's difficult to get students to start working. One of the main reasons for this is that students become negative if they feel the work is either too easy or too difficult for them. This initial refusal to start can quickly spread around the class and can be very dispiriting for the teacher.

Start off with a multiple-choice sheet (which can be adapted to fit any subject area). This sheet should contain questions with at least three possible answers. Having a firm written task automatically settles the class. What's more, as the work is pitched at the right level it allows them to have a go straightaway. Once they're settled into this you can then introduce more challenging work.

THE BEAUTY OF CHOICE

IDEA

28

EXTRA HELP FOR YOU AND THEM

If some of your students are having problems getting started with a specific task, giving them an extra help sheet is a good idea. This sheet should break down the task into smaller chunks and, if necessary, contain a sample answer for them to copy to get them started.

It is well worth spending a fair bit of time designing 'user friendly' help sheets as they can be used as an effective support to normal teaching materials. Explain to the student that as they're having trouble starting you have prepared a special 'booster' for them. But don't give them out too easily, or everyone will want one!

This frees you up to circulate around the class and help others. When used carefully the extra help sheet is like having an additional assistant in the room with you.

Record an audio tape of a reading of a piece of text. Try to make it about five minutes long and either record your own voice or, even better, that of a colleague. Prepare a copy of the text as a handout and give this to the class. Play the tape asking the students to follow it on their handout.

The change of hearing a recorded voice, instead of you speaking, really interests students. This also allows you to keep your eyes on the class and make non-verbal signs to keep them listening, rather than concentrating on reading yourself.

If you refer to a visual, at that point in the tape you can hold it up to show the class, which also heightens their interest.

Students also love to hear music. If you can find a piece that's relevant to the lesson, play it to conclude. You will find this lesson really sticks in your students' minds.

USING AN AUDIO TAPE

IDEA
30

THE 'SELF-CONTAINED' LESSON

It is very tempting to carry a lesson directly on from the last one. However, you might find some problems arising from this. Materials you wanted your students to bring just don't appear. Or students may be at various stages of completion, so it can be difficult to restart the lesson and keep up the momentum.

If, however, you start a new and different lesson each time you can lose the sense of continuity. So aim to make your lessons completely self-contained to get your students starting on the work together. This work should, however, link with your previous lesson. As the lesson progresses you can bring in further links from the last lesson where appropriate. This gets over the problem of those who missed the previous lesson and it allows keen students to revisit their work to finish it off or expand it. The beauty of this is that you achieve the best of both worlds: continuity and an organized restart.

Changing activities within a lesson can often cause problems. Some students will want to carry on with what they're doing and the teacher will be strongly tempted to just let the activity drift on as it's easier that way.

However, a good way to change activities is to use a 'buffer' or a 'bridge' activity. It will round off the last piece of work, raise interest levels and kick start the new section of the lesson.

Ask for a volunteer to come to the front and tell the class three key things about the area of study you have just been working on. I find there's always one who will come up to do this. The fact that someone new (other than you) is at the front seems to grab the class's attention. If the student gets stuck, either ask for one other student to come up and help out, or offer to help yourself. Use this to conclude the work just done and then present the next activity.

BRIDGING ACTIVITIES

It is essential to learn techniques that provide smooth transition from one activity to another. Following on from Idea 31, here are some more tips.

Students will get used to a clear signal and a clear routine. For example, ask them to stop writing and then wait, repeating the request if necessary, until they have. Now you can give your instructions. Remember to keep them clear, short and to the point. Have a visual back up which you can point to. Repeat your instructions clearly, then have a 'trigger' phrase like: 'Ok let's move onto the new activity now. Stop the old one or we'll run out of time!'

You will find that as long as the materials they need are well organized and your visual back up is prominent, together with a strong clear routine, then the students will get used to changing activities smoothly. It will raise efficiency and reduce stress.

Sometimes it's a good idea to give your class a break. If given now and again, and timed well, it's brilliant. Don't overdo it though, as they'll come to expect it every lesson.

If the students have done well, tell them so and give them three minutes to chat quietly while preparing for the next task. Once the time is up have a strong signal to let them know the next task is beginning. The students will appreciate that you're trying to help them and they'll cooperate. Make two important conditions for the break:

1 Noise must be kept to a reasonable level.
2 The students must pay attention when the new task starts.

THE BRILLIANT 'BREAK'

IDEA

34

THE SECRET OF PACE

A common problem for teachers is the speed at which they operate. It is natural with 30 people demanding your attention to respond quickly to get everyone's problems sorted. Remember that the demand on your time in the lesson will always vastly outstrip your ability to sort everything out. If you go too fast, two negative things will happen.

1   You will burn yourself out.
2   The quality of your teaching is reduced because of the speed at which it's delivered.

To try and avoid this:

○   make it a habit to ask yourself, from time to time, whether you're going too fast;
○   do things one at a time and at a steady pace;
○   refuse to be interrupted when you are giving individual help;
○   remind the students that you're trying to help everyone but you can only do one thing at a time.

You will find that you'll be left with more energy and your students will actually learn more from you.

A good way of reinforcing a particular message about behaviour in the classroom is to have well-presented posters around your walls. These confirm what you're saying when you remind a student of an important ground rule. If, for example, a student keeps calling out, remind them of the 'hands up rule' and then point to a poster which refers to it. This has a far greater impact and effectively gets your point across.

VISUAL REINFORCEMENT

BEHAVIOUR TRACKING CHARTS

For this system to work it must be kept simple and followed up in every lesson.

Towards the end of the lesson allocate a behaviour code to each student. This can be done in a positive and upbeat way. I find four categories work well. For example:

○ dark green = room for improvement;
○ blue = satisfactory;
○ orange = good;
○ yellow = excellent.

Sum up quickly towards the end of the lesson (reminders during the lesson) and say things like:

○ 'Darren, you have definitely improved with your behaviour today, you get Orange.'
○ 'Wayne, I must say I'm a bit disappointed and you know why. I've got to give you Dark Green.'

Follow up by having a large chart on the wall with the students' names clearly displayed down the left-hand side. Each lesson colour in the boxes so that everyone's behaviour and progress is there for all to see. You will be pleasantly surprised to find that the students will want to earn a good behaviour colour and that they'll compete with each other. Keep this simple and straightforward, attend to it every lesson and draw attention to it regularly. Explain that copies go to the head of subject and are used at parents' evenings. Indeed, individual records can easily be sent home each half term.

A good idea for keeping up the self-esteem of students over a long period of time is to use 'Best work and achievement folders'. Clearly label each folder with the name of each student and keep them in the classroom at all times.

Encourage students to put particularly good pieces of work into their folder. If something good happens to them, or they are proud of something, encourage them to make a note of it and pop it in the folder. You may find that it takes a fair bit of persistence on your part to get this system up and running, but with patience it will more than repay your initial efforts.

When the student has low self-esteem or motivation sit down for a few moments with them and go through the folder. It does have an uplifting effect. Over time the students will be pleasantly surprised at how much is in there.

Be active in looking out for things that the student could include. In conversation with the student if you hear of something good, why not make a brief note and pop it in the folder? It gives a strong message to the student that you're encouraging them to do well.

BEST WORK AND ACHIEVEMENT FOLDERS

IDEA 38

Managing a discussion can sometimes seem impossible, especially when students all call out at the same time and don't listen to one another.

An easy and effective method to manage a discussion is to arrange the class into four teams, each with a nominated captain. Write on the board the names of the team captains with room for recording any points scored or deducted. The captain must choose who speaks from their team (obviously make sure that this is fair). The teams get a point if they contribute a constructive comment to the discussion. And each time someone calls out without permission, a point is deducted from their team score. The competitive element keeps the classroom on track.

Insist that the students put their hands up when they wish to ask questions or contribute to discussions.

A common problem is that a student puts up his or her hand and then speaks anyway. So, it's a good idea to designate times in the lesson when you're quite clear that you don't want anybody to put their hand up as everybody should be listening. If somebody puts their hand up during that time, stop and remind them of your rule. You will find that if you stick rigidly to this the students will get used to, and comply with, your system.

To reinforce this, make it a habit to congratulate students who stick to the protocol. Continue to reprimand those who break the rule and praise those who keep to it and you will gradually win the class round.

THE HANDS UP REMINDER

IDEA 40

When you give instructions or ask questions of the students, build in a period of time for them to take in what you've said or asked. Become an expert on the timing of this. Don't always pick the first hand that goes up. Give the students thinking time and encourage more to put their hands up.

This issue of timing is crucial in getting the best from your students.

TIME FOR INSTRUCTIONS

If you ask a question you often find that the usual 'few' will put up their hands and the usual 'many' will not. Often the ones who put up their hands can use their body language and voice to command attention. They are used to repeating this pattern in every lesson. So, it's a good idea to alternate the way in which you ask your class questions.

For example, give the students a spare piece of paper each. Ask a question and allow a few moments for them to jot down an answer on the paper. Encourage them to have a go even if they're not sure. Then you can ask them what they've written on the paper, or walk round the room and just look at the answers. This is a useful alternative to the hands up approach and involves more of the students without embarrassing them.

DEALING WITH THE WRONG ANSWER

If you ask your class a question, there will always be some students who answer incorrectly. The challenge is how to react to this. For example, if you say 'Good' to encourage them, then you can cause confusion because the answer is wrong. If you say 'No, that's not the right answer,' you could dampen their confidence and they may not contribute any more. It is important to create an atmosphere where the wrong answer is welcome.

The key is to make sure all the students participate. You could say something like: 'I see what it is you're thinking. Well done for trying. That's not the correct answer this time. Try again in a minute though, won't you?' Give them an encouraging smile and move on.

You could use instances of when famous people got it wrong, for example: 'Edison produced hundreds of "wrong" light bulbs before he achieved success.'

Continuing the theme of Idea 41, questions can be tailored to make them a fair and useful experience for everyone. Below is an example of questioning that I've used to great effect to get whole-class participation.

Give out coloured cards, apparently at random, to all members of the class. Tell them that their cards are for them to jot down answers and that you've also put some clues on the back. You now have groups of students each with the same colour. But beforehand you've decided which student will have which colour card. With the help of your seating plan and the way the cards are sorted you can quickly give them out to the right students.

The idea is this – you've worked out the ability of each student and the clues on the back of the cards are tailored to support their particular ability range. For example, the clue on one colour card may say: 'Question 1: The capital of France is Par_ _' for the less able. For the more able, maybe: 'The capital of France is _ _ _ _ _? (Clue: it has the Eiffel Tower)', and so on.

Now when you ask questions you can turn it into a fun game, for example: 'Question 1, what is the capital of France? Only the yellow cards may answer this one. If you get stuck look on the back of the card for clues.'

This way you can control who answers and you can support each student's answer without actually saying anything. The system ensures that everyone can join in.

IDEA 44

USING THE BEST IDEAS FROM OTHER SUBJECTS

A great strategy for dealing with challenging behaviour is to exchange the techniques that work well in other subject areas. Teachers tend to get trapped within their own department and short-sightedness can creep in. A wider perspective can be very helpful.

In practical terms arrange a meeting, say every couple of months, with teachers from other subject areas and find out what special strategies for behaviour control they employ. A lot of these can be easily adapted for use in your subject area. It's even better to observe other lessons to see how an idea works.

Ideas that I've seen work to great effect are listed below.

○ In physical education a five minute physical warm-up session is used. Why not use that in your subject, to kick start the brain?

○ In technology the teacher may have a cabinet with marked places for all the tools to go back to before anyone can be dismissed. A similar idea could be employed to get the equipment back in other subjects to save end of lesson searches and arguments. Any help with organization efficiency automatically helps with managing behaviour.

○ In Drama the command 'freeze' is often used. This could be very useful!

The more ideas you have the better, and the great thing is that other teachers have already tried and tested their ideas for you and the students are used to going along with them.

Many teachers have had the horrific experience of a physical fight between two students in their classroom. When analysing what happened you almost always find that if the teacher had intervened earlier he or she could have stopped the fight before it started.

It's a good idea to develop a 'nose' for a particular type of behaviour between students which signals there's trouble ahead, and you must always be on the lookout for it. Adopt a no-nonsense approach. If, for example, they ignore your requests to stop the name calling then you ask one of them to step outside the room and call for assistance.

With practice you will identify the type of banter which is normal for a particular group, and aggressive behaviour which, if left unchecked, could easily escalate into a fight. It is quite rare but when it happens it must be dealt with by early, brisk and firm intervention.

PREVENTING FIGHTS

Sometimes a lesson will go so badly that the teacher feels he or she has completely lost control and will dread seeing that class again.

Try and deal with a really bad lesson in a systematic and logical way. The worse thing to do is to carry on the next lesson as if nothing has happened. If you do that the same problems will be back to haunt you.

Try asking for help. Run through what you attempted to do and how it all went wrong with your head of department or a senior teacher. Action should be seen to be taken the very next lesson. So, start the next lesson with a senior teacher in the room and with the ring leaders isolated in a discipline support supervision room. If possible, arrange for that teacher to stay the whole lesson. If that can't be arranged then try to get somebody to help you at the start and end of the lesson. Having another teacher there shows the students that they're not just taking you on but the whole teaching network.

The next lesson with the class who seriously played you up is very important. The objective of this lesson is for you to regain full control of the situation and the class. At the start explain briefly what went wrong. For example:

> *'Obviously last lesson wasn't good. A lot of students ignored my instructions. Some of the main students who did are not with this group today because of that. I want good behaviour today so that we can all carry on learning. That is why we are here.'*

Make sure that the work for this lesson is very clear and straightforward. Remember, the chief objective is to regain control. You will find the lesson will go well but don't become complacent. You still have to reintegrate the ring-leaders back into your group (see Idea 47).

This idea follows on from Idea 46, where troublesome ring leaders have been isolated from the class. The best way to reintegrate them is with senior management support. You can try bringing them back one by one over a series of lessons, or maybe two at a time. The important thing is to show the student that their previous behaviour was totally unacceptable. It crossed your 'bottom line'.

You can then continue with your lessons using all the techniques and ideas outlined in this book. A particular focus could be to perhaps let little things go so as to not aggravate the situation. You will find that by using this method the lesson will return to a manageable level. If you still encounter serious recurrent problems with the same students, there may be a strong case for an exchange with other groups.

REINTEGRATING RING LEADERS

IDEA

48

TACKLING TESTS

In teaching you need to test your students in order to see how much they've learnt. But the problem is there are just too many tests and naturally students get fed up with them. The word 'test' sets up the wrong associations, so try calling them something different. Phrases that have worked well for me are:

○ fun 'feed back' sessions;
○ 'how much can you remember?' sessions;
○ 'impress me with your knowledge in just ten minutes' sessions.

Use your imagination to present tests in a positive light and you'll find students are much more willing.

Setting and collecting in homework for a challenging group can become a nightmare.

Set a piece of written homework with at least a week or more in which to do it. This gives you time to collect it in and then remind the stragglers when it's due. Make a big deal of that one written piece. Another reminder can be given at the next lesson. Spare instructions can be on hand.

If homework is still missing keep back the culprits. Explain that you've reminded them three times and if it's not in next lesson a lunchtime detention will be set. Follow through with the lunchtime detention as a last resort.

Only when that piece of homework is fully sorted out for all students in the class do you progress to the next piece of homework. This gives the strong signal that homework is important, that they have plenty of time and reminders and that you won't give up. You are also allowing yourself more time for chase ups and organization.

MAKING HOMEWORK MORE MANAGEABLE

Be creative when setting homework. Ask your students to do something related to their own interests and to give some quick oral feedback in the next lesson. For example, ask them to prepare a quick summary of their favourite hobby or pastime. You can alternate this type of homework with the more formal written request.

By being creative, the students will enjoy it more and it will therefore be easier to manage.

SETTING FUN HOMEWORK

Marking books can be a time consuming activity. With students with challenging behaviour the sad truth is that they often don't even read the comments you have spent hours writing. So, a good idea is to develop a quick-fire system that is rapid enough for you to mark the entire set of books after each lesson. It won't take you long but it really benefits the students.

Have separate scales for effort, output and quality and give them marks out of ten for each of these. You could also have a chart on the wall on which you display the results lesson by lesson. (You can have a more thorough and detailed mark on a periodic basis, for example once a fortnight.) The beauty of the quick-fire system is that you can give feedback quickly and efficiently at the start of the lesson about how they did in the last lesson. There are lots of advantages with this quick-fire system, for example:

o there's a built in target-setting process which is simple and effective;
o students have fast feedback;
o students know each lesson that you're going to definitely look at their work and this makes them work better;
o simplified responses are easy to understand.

The key point is to keep the system simple to use so you can maintain a consistent approach across each term.

Although the below takes a bit of organizing it will pay back huge dividends in the next lesson and throughout the term. Write down on a large sheet of paper two clear points about the next lesson under the headings:

1 This is what we are going to do next lesson.
2 This is why we are going to do it.

Remember to keep it clear and simple. Then ask the students to think about how you are going to tackle the task. A huge advantage is the consistency this gives at the start of the next lesson. Show them the sheet with the outline and repeat it. You will find that if you make a habit of this (which doesn't take long) it registers that you are organized and that there is a clear structure to the work. It sends strong signals to your students that you know exactly what you're doing.

CONTROLLING THE END OF A LESSON

Dealing with common problems

IDEA 53

HELPING INDIVIDUALS

It is very frustrating for a teacher to be faced with a request to help a student who clearly needs it, and yet not be able to do so because the noise levels and disruption of the class increase as soon as the students know that they're not being watched.

So how do you manage this situation? A good idea is to call the student up to your desk, get him or her to stand to one side so that you can look at his or her work and discuss it while still watching the class. As you look at the work keep commenting on individuals in the class. This works well because the class will hear these comments and know that everyone is under your watchful gaze!

It is a great idea to build up a good network of contacts at your school so that you can arrange for other teachers to pop in and support you, even if it's only for a few minutes at the beginning and end of lessons.

You can arrange to return the favour in your free periods. This is a great investment.

GETTING SUPPORT

THE STRATEGIC BLIND EYE

One of the tensions with challenging behaviour is maintaining a balance between getting the lesson flowing and not allowing unruly students to behave exactly as they like.

It is easy to get into confrontational situations and get involved in energy sapping rows (your energy, not theirs). On top of this, other students are ready to pounce if they see anything other than fair play!

Think of your lesson as a carriage on a journey. Make sure you fit your wheels with 'springs' to absorb the little annoying things. Without the springs you can find yourself reacting to every jolt along the way. A lot of those little jolts can be tactically ignored. (I've touched on this briefly in Idea 47.) However, be strategic in your approach – if something is important then you should deal with it. This approach saves you energy and keeps the lesson flowing better. In a nutshell, see everything that is going on but only react to selected things.

Some students appear friendly, polite and cooperative but do not complete any work. They may well make token efforts but they're really not working at all. There is a huge temptation with a challenging group to let these students get away with it. After all, they're not holding you up from teaching the rest. You must, however, make sure that you tackle this one. If you don't two serious problems will occur. First, the student will be entrenched in the habit of doing no work, and if this is allowed it will become virtually impossible to get him or her to work and she therefore won't learn much. Second, many of the students will have a great excuse not to work, citing him or her as an example.

Therefore, keep chipping away and monitor how much he or she is doing by setting step-by-step targets. Explain that he or she is a very pleasant student but that he or she is there is to learn. In most cases, when students realize you won't give up they start to work.

BULLYING IN THE CLASSROOM

If you see that students are repeatedly making unkind comments to another student then you must give warnings for the behaviour to stop and a report must be sent to the head of year straight away.

If the comments continue, remove all of the students who ignore your instructions to a discipline support room immediately. (Use senior teacher back up for this.) Make sure the situation is resolved before you allow those particular students to join the next lesson (see Idea 47). Failure to respond firmly and quickly to this situation can have devastating results.

The golden rule is do not, under any circumstances, be dragged into an argument with a student in the classroom. The fact that you're arguing with them shows that they have control of the situation. If you do make the mistake of arguing with the student this can easily ruin a lesson.

Instead, ask them to see you after the lesson and then focus straight back to the work in hand. If the student persists (and they often will) calmly repeat that you will not argue in the classroom. Be very firm. In most cases this will solve the problem as the student will realize that their ploy to disrupt has failed. But, if the student persists in an argument after all reasonable steps have been taken, then you must arrange to have that student removed immediately (see Idea 54).

IDEA 59

Teachers often enjoy talking about something they're particularly interested in but which isn't relevant to the lesson, for example an 'alien'. Once students are aware of a teacher's pet subject they will often bring it up in order to get out of doing any work. Guard against this. Be aware of this and try instead to say: 'I'd love to talk about this. Come and see me at the end of the lesson.' Then direct all the attention back to the matter in hand.

HOW TO TACKLE THE MENACE OF 'ALIENS'

Everybody likes a bargain. You can use this fact to great effect when trying to encourage students to work. If they are not getting on with it, or have stopped working, you can suggest a smaller, easier task for them to do. Or you could offer to cancel a detention.

If applied with firm humour this method will produce great cooperation. For this to work well, have quiet conversations with individual students. A word of warning – don't be too easy to negotiate with!

THE POWER OF THE 'BARGAIN'

MOVING STUDENTS

Moving students can present problems. You ask a student to move and they refuse. What do you do? The whole class is watching. Do you get into an argument that you may well lose? First of all refer to 'The golden rules of seating plans' (Idea 86).

Here is what to do. Make sure the student has had several warnings. If, however, he or she continues to ignore your requests, walk over to the seat you want him or her to move to and pull it away from the desk. Then walk over to the student and hold one open hand towards him or her (with a distance of about half a metre) and with the other hand pointing to the other seat and repeat your request. Then wait, remembering to stay calm. The student at this point may argue with you, however simply repeat your instructions, this time adding: 'I'm trying to get on with teaching my class; you're holding me up. I'm waiting.' Be calm and keep your voice low and firm.

If he or she still doesn't move then repeat the instructions again. It's surprising how often a student will actually move at this point. There is strong psychological pressure at work here. In the rare cases when the student still won't move, then say: 'Right, I'm not wasting any more time with this. I will see you at the end of this lesson. I need to continue teaching my class.' Continue teaching and make sure you do see the student at the end and that a sanction is given, for example time out from the next lesson.

A big problem with students with challenging behaviour is their insistence on not wearing the school uniform correctly. You can choose to ignore it, although this could make the situation worse. Or you can choose to challenge the students and end up with arguments and serious disruption at the start of a lesson. So what do you do?

A good idea is to make the request to the whole class. As the lesson progresses carry on doing what you have planned but give reminders to the students who are still ignoring your instructions regarding the uniform. Make those reminders 'slip in' with the teaching but don't make them confrontational. After ten or 15 minutes, take out a notebook and say: 'Right, I'm not going to spend all lesson being ignored about the uniform. Those who are still ignoring me will have your names written in this book and you'll be dealt with by the head of year.'

Then begin to write their names in the book. You will be pleasantly surprised at how many will now comply with the uniform code. For those who still do not, have a quiet little mention to them at the end of the lesson and make sure that the head of year follows up with the school's sanction for incorrect dress code. If the student does not comply in the next lesson you'll have to arrange to have him or her isolated from your next lesson. It is a good idea to tell the class why this is being done. In this way the other students see that you mean what you say.

UNIFORM

MOBILE PHONES

This is a very common distraction for students. Check the guidelines your school has set down regarding mobile phones and make sure you are consistent in following them.

It can be very difficult to take phones from students. Try walking up to them, putting your hand out and asking politely but firmly for the phone. The student will go through the motions of putting the phone away. But it will come back a few seconds later. So you wait and then repeat your request but add that you'll put it in the cupboard and show the key for emphasis. There is something about this approach which makes the student think you really mean business. Although they may not hand you the phone you will find that it will not come out again.

It may be useful to refer back to Idea 19 here, as it asks you to think in advance about your reactions to common problems such as this.

Some behaviour problems are caused by the perception students have of always doing the same thing in your lessons. If they feel they're heading towards a dreary routine lesson, they will be uninterested in what you have to say before they even get to you!

To counteract this, surprise students with variety. Below is a sample of some of the many things you can try:

- go to the back of the room to talk to them so that they have to turn round;
- get them to stand up and gather around you as you show them a picture;
- have a TV programme playing on the video as they come in (it may be a theme connected to the lesson). Don't explain anything at the first stage just put a finger to your mouth and signal for them to sit quietly.
- hand them an envelope each as they come in which is sealed (it might have the starter in it) and hold a large card which says 'don't open it yet!';
- have a present wrapped up (a good idea is a bar of chocolate inside a big box covered in bright wrapping paper) which you hold up to show them and a sign which says: 'this present will be given to the quietest student at the end of the lesson!'

Variations will really command the attention of your students and get them looking forward to the next surprise in your lesson!

OVERCOMING THE RUT OF ROUTINES

'I HAVEN'T GOT A PEN'

This is so common and can be very irritating. If you have a ready supply of pens they soon disappear, and then where is the incentive for students to remember to bring a pen? On the other hand, not giving a spare pen can result in an even bigger problem as the student will use the absence of a pen to his or her full advantage to get out of doing any work.

A great idea is to have some pens ready with bright sticky tape on them in various colours. Make a point of reminding the student you'll need a word after the others have gone, and write the name of the student and the colour of the spare pen on the board. This ensures two things: first, you get your pen back and second, you've made your point and kept the flow of the lesson going without the student getting away with it.

It takes a small amount of preparation but this simple idea will bring a smooth solution to this common problem.

'We've already done this!' is another common phrase. This one can unnerve teachers quite easily. You must remain calm and not look surprised. Do not argue about whether or not they have done this particular piece of work before. Instead you can claim several very good reasons for repeating work. I've listed a few below.

○ You're looking at the same topic but from a different angle.
○ It's a very large topic and so a lot of time needs to be spent on it.
○ It's a difficult concept and so needs to be done more than once.
○ It's revision.

'I'M NOT FEELING WELL!'

'I'm not feeling well!' is a tricky phrase to deal with. Monitor the situation carefully to see how the student is as the lesson progresses. You have to use your professional judgement to decide how genuine the case is. If they will not work after ten minutes, tell him or her that either they work or they must go to the medical room.

Sometimes a student will refer to another teacher regarding work they're doing in another class. Be very careful here. The student may criticize the teacher and try to goad you into agreeing. You must act decisively. Make a comment like: 'It is unprofessional to discuss other members of staff' and direct attention back to the task in hand. In most cases this will stop the problem.

If the student persists then you must treat it as a clear disciplinary matter. Remind the student more firmly that it is extremely impolite to continue with such comments and if necessary have the student removed from the room. In practice it is rare for it to reach this stage.

TALKING ABOUT ANOTHER TEACHER

IDEA

69

THE TEENAGE 'CRUSH'

It is a strange fact that students can develop a 'crush' on a teacher. You must be sensitive about this and usually after a short time it will pass. However, maintain meticulous professional conduct and if the student hangs around to speak to you on a regular basis for no apparent reason then arrange for another teacher to speak to them. If the student writes a personal note to you, whatever the content, it must be immediately referred to your line manager. Continue to treat the student as you normally would until the crush disappears.

If a student makes an abusive comment to you in the street, never deal with it there and then. Take it up next time you're at school with senior teachers.

The best way to deal with it is to arrange an early meeting to stop the situation getting out of control. The meeting should be with you, the senior teacher, the student and his or her parents or guardians. It must be explained that the matter is very serious. The school's ethos about polite behaviour extends outside the school as well. It must be made clear to the student that further abusive comments in the street will not be tolerated under any circumstances.

Make a file note of the incident for the record. It is best to end the meeting with a tone of forgiveness and reconciliation. Continue to treat the student as you would have done and make no further reference to the incident.

If, in rare cases, the abusive behaviour continues in the street rely on the school's system. Never try to deal with it as an individual.

Giving out sanctions and rewards

IDEA 71

THE DETENTION LETTER

Very often a teacher, frustrated with a student's behaviour, will resort to issuing a detention. That seems straightforward enough, however there are at least five major drawbacks to giving a detention.

1 It can often cause resentment immediately and make the situation worse.
2 You are involved in a round of form filling which can take up a lot of valuable time.
3 You must go through the follow-up process of checking that the student attended the detention (it is quite common for the student not to turn up).
4 If the student doesn't turn up then you either have to ignore it, in which case the whole system falls down, or get involved in yet more administration work re-appointing the detention.
5 Detentions are often a cause of arguments with parents.

I am not suggesting for one moment that the detention system should be scrapped. As a last resort it can be an extremely useful sanction. There is however a better way to deal with things. Try having a 'formal detention warning' letter (as laid out below) as a buffer before entering the detention zone.

The 'Formal Detention Warning' letter
'Despite reminders from the teacher to keep
to the school rules the conduct of

_____

has continued to be un-cooperative. Notice
is hereby given that if the situation of non
cooperation continues arrangements will be put
in place for a detention in Room _____
on _____.

(Signed by the teacher)
copies to Head of Department.'

I always make a big deal when I issue one of these.
Write the student's name in a book checking with
them who their form tutor is and then you hand
them the warning.

I have found that this works wonders. Students like
to have 'an escape route' and you will find that
often, after initial protests, the student's behaviour
will improve, and they will be anxious to confirm
with you that their behaviour is better by the end
of the lesson. The beauty of the idea is that it
involves the teacher in minimal work compared to
a detention and yet it produces better results.

TARGETING THE RING LEADERS

It is tempting to react to a really bad lesson by punishing the whole class; after all it seemed like the whole class messed about. This is always a mistake. Instead, discern who the ring leaders are and make sure you only punish them. In a class of 25 you may find about five or seven ring leaders. It is not an exact science, but as a rule of thumb an average class of challenging behaviour will have a third who are comparatively easy to manage, a third who will mess around given the right conditions and a hardcore third of ring leaders.

I have observed new teachers with challenging classes. As their control of the class comes under threat they issue lots of sanctions. It can quickly escalate, which is a horrible experience, as you begin to wonder what on earth you can do to make it stop. Thoughts of cleaning windows for a job become a vision of heaven at these times!

I have found that the 'ladder of consequences' works extremely well. For example, if a particular group of students is misbehaving you can say: 'Right, in a moment I'm afraid I am going to consider moving one of you.' Notice that all you are actually threatening is 'to consider' something. However, it's the teacher's tone of voice which sends strong psychological messages to the class as a whole. You are not going to lose face or be involved in the arguments which the giving of detentions can generate.

At the point when a sanction becomes necessary say: 'You leave me no choice, Martin, I'm writing your name in my book.' Notice that you're simply writing a name in a book! The written word seems to carry great authority and power. You put the book back into your pocket and direct attention straight back onto the lesson.

To sum up, don't give your most severe punishment first. Use a strong tone of voice, always direct attention back to the work and increase your threats slowly.

THE 'LADDER OF CONSEQUENCES'

PRAISING STUDENTS

When you're trying to settle a class it's tempting to always say negative things. The problem with this is that it sets up a confrontational atmosphere that almost always invites bad behaviour.

A better approach is to tell them off with praise. For example: 'Michael, you're the last person I would have thought would interrupt me, you normally listen so well.' If used carefully this will have a far better outcome.

Try motivating your challenging group by organizing a weekly raffle. The prize could be a bar of chocolate or a magic trick box (anything you think they'll like!). To be entered the students must maintain a good behaviour level throughout the week. You'll be surprised how well this works as students start to behave so as not to miss out on the fun.

You can add to the effectiveness by making little 'deals' where you agree to put their name back in the draw if they improve their behaviour straight away. It also creates a bit of welcome fun at the end of the week and helps foster better longer-term relationships between you and your students.

THE RAFFLE

Try to make sure that a punishment is proportional to the behaviour that led to it. For example, if you catch a student damaging your wall display, arrange for a short detention for him or her to come to your room and repair it. The student will see this as a fair consequence.

If a student is particularly unkind to another student then arrange for the student causing the problem to stay back for a short while to write a letter of apology. If a student forgets to bring in homework for a second time arrange for a lunchtime detention in which the student can complete the work. If, however, there is a serious problem, for example violent behaviour, then make sure that parents are brought into the school to urgently discuss the matter with a senior member of staff. If the students see that generally the punishment and response is fair and proportional the whole discipline system will work more efficiently and effectively.

Teaching is a long-term engagement and the development of consistent and effective habits will make your job easier. One is to build good relationships with your students. It is good to say things like: 'You're a pleasant lad, however, when you call out like that you're ignoring the school's rules. Please sort that out.' That is a far better way to reprimand a student than to say: 'You're always calling out. You're very annoying.'

As teachers we shouldn't forget that students' feelings work exactly like ours do as adults. If somebody criticizes us we naturally get defensive and it's no different for them.

Even when you need to give a serious sanction, like a detention, you can say

> *'It really is a shame Matthew. Most of the time you are fine, but that last lesson you decided to ignore all my instructions. Therefore you must do this detention, and then next lesson we'll get you back to normal.'*

In this way, the students will see that you're being fair in doing your job. This is a vital tip and will help you succeed in the long run.

SEPARATING BEHAVIOUR FROM THE STUDENT

IDEA 78

Have a supply of congratulation letters typed out on headed paper with a space for the student's name and a box to handwrite the specific area of work being praised. This means that the letter can be quickly written out in the lesson and handed to the student there and then. The immediacy of this reward makes it very effective. You can also say at the start of the lesson: 'Now, I have three letters to go home to praise you. Who is going to earn them?' This sets a challenge. Keep the letters to about three per lesson for maximum effect. Too many will devalue them.

Try to keep the treat of showing a video to
a minimum. If shown at the end of term, or after a
difficult unit of work, then it makes it appear more
of a treat. If you have a selection of videos it's best
to not ask the class which one they want. All this
will do is cause an argument that could wreck your
lesson. Instead, carefully choose one which you
think they'll like (the more up to date the better)
and just put it straight on. There will be protestors
but they'll settle down.

THE VIDEO TREAT

The big picture

IDEA

80

AFTER-SCHOOL CLUBS

A fantastic way to build great relationships with the students which also translates into better behaviour management is to start an 'after-school club'.

Have it on the same day each week and start it 15 minutes after the end of school for, say, 30–45 minutes. Constantly remind students about it and talk it up.

The purpose of the club is to give extra help and encouragement but make it fun. Have things to eat and drink, play music and keep the atmosphere relaxed.

I know that a lot of teachers scoff at such an idea and believe that such a club only works with well-behaved students. But if you try it out, organize it well, keep it going and have clear ground rules you'll find that a few students will come, and if they enjoy it, will get others to come. With students with challenging behaviour you can give more one-to-one individual help. The results can be truly amazing.

It is another way of showing the students you care and I have often had students show great disappointment when such a club is discontinued. Remember, for some of them the prospect of going home is not always that great.

Teaching assistants (TAs) are a fantastically useful resource in helping to deal with bad behaviour. Unfortunately, due to time restraints and all sorts of other reasons, it's common to find that TAs are not used effectively at all. It is important for a good strong professional bond to be established between you and your TA. Below are some golden rules to developing an effective partnership.

○ Make time to meet outside of the lesson to briefly outline strategies and approaches.
○ Develop a double act by rehearsing a set of 'what ifs' so that together you will have more confidence in your approach.
○ Don't forget to give your assistant a thumbnail outline of the lesson plan.
○ Allow and encourage your assistant to have the full authority for discipline that you have, and constantly remind your class of this.
○ If you have a particularly challenging student you may wish to sit your assistant next to that student to help focus him or her onto his or her work.
○ If you are reading to the class or demonstrating something, it's a good idea to get your TA to help with this as it's more interesting for the students to hear another voice and (not to mention) more interesting for the assistant too.
○ So with a little bit of planning and discussion you can develop a partnership with your assistant which will bring huge rewards when dealing with challenging behaviour.

TEACHING ASSISTANTS

USING VISITORS

Often with a challenging class teachers feel, quite naturally, that it's too risky to bring in a visitor. However, a fantastic way to help a challenging class is to actively arrange for other people to come in and do a presentation. For example: poets, folk singers, adventurers, professionals talking about their jobs, retired people reflecting on their lives, experts on a particular subject (e.g. UFOs), and so on. As you get more established at your school you can build up a network of contacts. The contacts can be local or people within the school.

There's something about the sense of occasion and the presence of the visitor to the room that really raises interest levels. Students always enjoy the surprise of someone new and you can be creative and inventive with the way you link the visitor to the work you're currently doing.

People are very often flattered to be asked and will spend a great deal of time and effort preparing without expecting anything in return other than the experience of presenting their topic. Often they will bring in things to display that raises the interest level of students even further. The main thing to bear in mind is to plan ahead and give your guest plenty of time to prepare in advance.

Why not also try involving members of the support staff? You may find, for example, that the head caretaker has been on a trip to Australia and has plenty to talk about on the different culture, cuisine and animals out there.

One of the really pleasant surprises in teaching is that the vast majority of parents and guardians will support the teacher in his or her efforts in dealing with challenging behaviour. The important thing to remember is to ask specifically for their support. A lot of teachers wait until parents' consultation day. The problem with this is that often you'll find the very parents you want to speak to will not be there.

If you experience challenging behaviour and it doesn't improve in response to your normal strategies, then phone the parents promptly. Time spent on this now will pay huge dividends in the future management of the problem. It helps if you can be very specific and play up the positive aspect. For example: 'Dean is on Level 4 and we are trying to get him to Level 5. He is nearly there.'

Outline the ways in which you've tried to tackle the problem, and remember to be careful with your words, as however badly behaved the child is, he or she is a precious treasure to the parent! Then ask for help from the parent. You might say: 'I think that we're agreed that we both want Dean to do well in his work. Could you think of anything that you could do that might reinforce my efforts?' In most cases the parent will be able to suggest a sanction that they can give at home to support you. At the end of the conversation don't forget to sum up what has been agreed like this:

> 'So Mrs Smith, I do appreciate your time with this. Just to confirm then, if Dean doesn't respond to reasonable requests to behave himself then you will consider keeping him at home in the evenings for up to a week. That's great. Thank you.'

This is a powerful advantage if you take the time to set it up.

CONTACT WITH PARENTS

I find it a useful and an even more powerful advantage if I confirm the conversation with parents in writing straight away, and then keep in contact with the parent until things improve. Then you can both celebrate the improvement which has been achieved.

A further point is to mention your arrangement with their parents in an encouraging way to the student without the rest of the class hearing. I find the end of the lesson as the others leave the room is a good time to briefly mention it. Say something like: 'Dean, I've spoken to your mum and she, like me, wants you to do well. I hope that by the end of this week we can send a letter to say that things are improving!' Keep it to that. Don't mention what the sanction is as this will lead to conflict.

If this is carefully organized and followed up consistently, it will result in a huge improvement to the situation.

How you set out your classroom has a vital impact on the control of your students' behaviour. Below are my golden rules:

○ make sure that with challenging students they're all seated facing your way;
○ if the group is small enough insist on one to a double desk;
○ keep ring leaders apart;
○ have enough space so that you can get to each desk easily;
○ make sure there is plenty of space between the board and the front row of desks;
○ keep areas around your cupboard and desk clear for ease of access;
○ make sure everything you need is to hand.

If you make sure these simple things are in place it will make your lesson much easier to manage.

THE CLASSROOM LAYOUT

THE GOLDEN RULES OF SEATING PLANS

Seating plans are an absolute necessity when dealing with a challenging group. Here are my golden rules.

1 When initially preparing the seating plan, make sure the seats are laid out as you want them. Keep the more demanding students away from each other. Make sure that special needs are catered for. For example, a student with poor eyesight will need to be at the front.

2 If the group is small enough, insist on one student per double desk.

3 Ensure that the first few lessons are successful in getting students to sit at their allocated places. If it requires senior teacher assistance to enforce this in the early stages then so be it. This is a battle that must be won. It is better that students are taken out of the class than to allow them to sit where they wish.

4 Have copies of the seating plan typed up. You can have an enlarged copy put up on the wall with the name of the class boldly above it.

The students will ask to move and this can seem innocent enough. A vast variety of reasons are offered. At all costs resist the request to move seat. If you agree to one move I assure you that you will find a case of 'musical chairs' each lesson and the situation will worsen. In the end the students will sit wherever they please. Be cruel to be kind.

If a student gets out of his or her seat without permission make sure you ask him or her to return to it immediately. Absolutely insist that the students stay in their seats during a lesson. Reinforce this all the time. It is amazing how much trouble and disruption can be traced back to students leaving their seats when they please.

There is no reason why a student should need to get up without permission. If for example, it's to sharpen a pencil, sharpen it for them. Alongside this, make sure you have excellent systems for handing out and collecting in work to minimize the need for students to wander about (for tips on this see Idea 25).

KEEPING STUDENTS IN THEIR SEATS

IDEA

88

Now and again it's necessary to move a group from one room to another. This could be to use the library or a computer room. In the case of a very challenging group there is one golden rule: don't do it!

If it's unavoidable to use another room then it should be arranged in advance and the students need to be told to go to the new room instead of the old room in the next lesson. Have the door to the old room locked at the beginning of the lesson and arrange assistance. You will need to be stationed at the new room and another teacher must be outside the locked door of the old room reminding students where they should be. It's a good idea to never have a lesson which starts in one room and then is moved to another.

This is a very basic point but it's amazing how many teachers forget to comply with it. If you're telling off or praising a student at the end of the lesson when the rest of the class have gone, you must always have another student, teacher or teaching assistant in the room with you. This is common sense and must not be forgotten. In the absolute vast majority of cases it will be unnecessary, but it must be done to protect you against the potential of a false allegation of misconduct.

IDEA

90

Rather than school being teachers versus students it should be that teachers and students work together to progress with the work. This is the underlying philosophy behind the ideas in this book.

It is a good idea to frequently remind students about why you're asking them to stick to the protocols. This helps in getting them to comply because they see the sense in it, rather than just being told what to do. It also helps to show that you really are on their side.

Managing yourself

THE TWO TIMETABLES

It is easy to stick to the school timetable. However, a lot of teachers work long hours on preparation, marking, etc. In the long run this will wear you down. So it's a good idea to make a second timetable for your work outside of classroom hours.

It works particularly well if you take specific jobs, for example marking, preparing lessons, administration and anything unexpected, and allocate them specific times. For example: Mondays 4–5pm – mark Year 8 exercise books; Tuesday 4–5pm – do all outstanding admin work, and so on.

The main advantage to this system is that if you're meticulous and stick to it, any potential worry is removed and your spare time is freed up for you to enjoy yourself and recharge your batteries.

You cannot predict all the tasks that you do but if you keep a good record of how you spend your time over a period of a month it helps you to plan accurately and allocate tasks for future planning.

An important part of this arrangement is to be tough on yourself. If you have a set of books to mark in one hour then divide up the time by the amount of books and spend a certain amount of time on each book and no more. Otherwise a job has a habit of expanding to fill more time than it should.

It is a horrible experience to go to bed feeling that important tasks remain unfinished and with a sense of confusion about what must be done first. The idea for the 'second timetable' takes away this horrible experience and replaces it with a sense of being in control of your time, work and life.

You will never get everything done – ask any teacher! So, to help with organizing your priorities make a list of things to do under three headings:

A Must do.
B Should do.
C Would be nice to do.

Group the tasks into categories. For example, marking; planning; preparation of lessons; preparation of resources; and administration.

Make sure that you have a clear idea of the minimum requirements for the job and a clear view of your 'job description'. It is a good idea at this stage to get an experienced teacher in your subject area to look at your list and comment on it. Then make sure that all the minimum requirements of your job are marked with an 'A' category. Once category 'A' items are done then, and only then, do category 'B' items and then category 'C' items.

PRIORITIES

RELAXATION

Watch any teacher and you'll see them burning adrenaline like rocket fuel. So, on a daily basis make an appointment with yourself to relax. Ask your family not to disturb you. Once it becomes a habit stick to it come what may.

It might also be a good idea to go to relaxation classes to learn techniques about how to relax. And difficult though it is, cut down on tea and coffee and substitute with fruit juice and water. I find this greatly helps relaxation.

It is particularly important in teaching to become an expert on relaxation techniques during your working day. Many teachers are always on edge and this puts the students on edge.

Here are a couple of simple techniques which work very well:

○ clench your fists tightly for a count of seven and then relax them. Repeat this a few times and feel the tension ebb away;

○ be conscious of your breathing and make it become deep, slow and steady. Just ten breaths of this sort can calm you;

○ make sure you walk around as much as possible, in the classroom and between lessons. This is a great stress buster.

Choose a form of exercise and do it for one hour three times a week. No excuses! Your family will soon get used to your 'recharge' routine. I find the best types of exercise are those that are not fiercely competitive. For example: dancing, cycling, walking, swimming, golf and yoga.

Find the one that suits you and your lifestyle. The main thing to remember is to do regular small sessions that you can keep up the whole year round. That way you will get the best stress-busting benefit.

To encourage yourself, maintain a logbook of your exercise. Over time you'll find yourself trying to improve on your previous weekly total.

Slow and steady exercise works well. For example, you can learn Tai Chi. This exercise allows you to clear your mind, reduces muscle tension and gives you an enhanced sense of well-being.

Remember, whichever exercise you decide on, stick with it. The benefits to you and your job will be enormous.

YOUR EVENING

Have one evening a week in which you do your own thing. This can be anything as long as it's not connected to work. I find a Friday is best. Giving your mind a rest is essential for stress relief and for promoting peace of mind. After a while you'll look forward to this special break for yourself. There is something about taking your mind off of your job on a regular basis that is deeply satisfying. When you return to work you will feel more refreshed and balanced.

If you can get involved in something that has a social aspect, but with people who are not teachers, you will find that it broadens your horizons and allows you to see yourself in a wider perspective. It can be a refreshing break and good fun to regularly meet with a group where you share common interests.

By having one evening a week it can be regarded as a well-earned reward for working hard.

Why not join an evening class and learn something new? It is fantastic as a teacher to be able to cross the line and become a student. Psychologically it does you wonders and I've found that going to evening classes and discovering new subjects is a great joy.

Teachers are always giving out information and therefore it's good to have new information and ideas coming in. Another advantage to an evening class is that it develops your circle of friends to include those who are not teachers.

Another advantage is that you'll find your self-esteem increases as you learn new areas of knowledge. I particularly suggest joining a class where you learn something unusual or new to you. It is amazing how the new learning experience will activate parts of your mind that you forgot you had.

BECOMING A STUDENT AGAIN

SLOWING THE PACE

Teaching a class of demanding children has a profoundly draining effect on you. When you're in the classroom they're at you all the time. You have to be on your toes and on peak performance. Building on Ideas 93, 94 and 95, it's a good idea to make a conscious effort to slow down and ease any tension once outside the classroom. For example, slow your steps when you walk and think about the rhythm and pace of your breathing. When you eat, eat slowly, and remember to enjoy the food. When this turns into a lifestyle habit recharging your batteries will be so much easier!

To take away the guilt of not seeing friends as often as you should, schedule meeting them in the holidays and spread it out around the year. Your friends will soon get to know your reasons. I have known teachers who go through agonies trying to fit everyone in. While it's great to have colleagues who become friends, it's also good to keep in contact with friends who aren't teachers. You realize that there's more to life than just teaching issues!

As you might not see your friends as much you'd like to, why not make the occasions when you do see them particularly special.

Some suggestions are:

○ paying Cluedo dressed up in character;
○ murder mystery events;
○ paintballing;
○ medieval banquets;
○ theatre trips;
○ general knowledge evenings.

They may take time to organize but the fun you'll have will give you pleasant memories for years!

IDEA

99

A WARM BATH

Take a warm bath before you go to bed and read a light-hearted book. Even better is to light a candle and in the soft light listen to a favourite CD. Falling asleep will be so much easier.

A lot of teachers are so committed to their work that they work late into the evening. It is essential to have a cut off time that you stick to. Plan your evening so that you do have time for a long relaxing soak in the bath.

Always remember that the more relaxed your evening is the more efficient you will be the next day. You will need that energy to tackle those challenging students!

Keep a daily record of what you have done in a simplified form. After school, spend a few minutes jotting down the main things you've accomplished. Include things you feel you've done well in.

Keep all appointments and plans in one diary, and all 'to do' items on one 'to do' list. The ideal situation is to have all this in the one notebook.

In teaching it is absolutely vital to be well organized. Make sure that all paperwork is carefully filed in a way in which you can find what you need quickly. It is well worth having a certain amount of time each day to keep your organization up to date.

A SIMPLE WORK LOG